Her-Story Unveiled

Women's History
Through the Eyes
of Native American
Resilience

Dr. Talitha Agan

COPYRIGHT NOTICE

Tally Nine Productions
Publishers Since 2022
Modesto, California

Agan, Talitha.
Her-Story Unveiled: Women's History
Through the Eyes of Native American
Resilience

TALLY NINE
Productions

TABLE OF

Contents

Introduction

Keeping Biases and Stereotypes in Check: A Look at Native American Women in Women's History

Navigating Change: Native American Women and the Columbian Exchange

The Matrilineal Pueblo: Journeying Through the Lives of Pueblo Women in the Southwest from Pre-Contact to Colonization

Negotiating Power: The Influence of Native American Women in Fur Trading Roles in Early Northeastern America

Revisiting Women's History: Decoding Bias in Champlain's Accounts of Huron Society

Iroquois Matriarchy: The Pinnacle of Female Political Power

The Real Pocahontas: Untangling Disney Myths, History, and Modern Native Women's Issues

Conclusion

Suggested Reading

Image Citations

Bibliography

About Me

INTRODUCTION

Welcome to an exploration of Women's History that highlights the experiences of Native American women in the "New World." Often overshadowed by mainstream narratives, their stories are rich with resilience, strength, and cultural significance. This book compiles well-researched articles that illuminate the pivotal roles, contributions, and lives of Native American women before and during European contact.

It seeks to dismantle longstanding biases and stereotypes, offering a nuanced and comprehensive examination of their early histories.

Historically, the stories of Native American women have been filtered through the lens of colonial oppressors, resulting in significant misrepresentations. This book seeks to critically evaluate and correct some of these narratives, presenting a more authentic portrayal that honors the agency and resilience of Indigenous women.

From the arrival of Europeans and the profound shifts brought about by the Columbian Exchange to the unique societal structures of the Pueblo and Iroquois, each chapter provides a focused look at different aspects of Native American women's lives and the immense changes they navigated.

You will encounter the diverse ways in which Native American women influenced early North American history, whether through their crucial roles in the fur trade or by maintaining matrilineal societies that celebrated female power and influence. The book also tackles the romanticized and often inaccurate portrayals of iconic figures like Pocahontas, peeling back layers of myth to reveal the complex realities of cultural conflict, identity, and representation.

By incorporating firsthand accounts, oral histories, and Indigenous perspectives, this work presents a more holistic and inclusive understanding of Women's History. It is not just a recounting of past events but a call to recognize the enduring legacy and contributions of Indigenous women in shaping the history of the United States. These articles remind us of the importance of recognizing and honoring the diverse stories of Native American women. Their narratives are integral to the broader understanding of Women's History. They offer valuable lessons in cultural awareness, resilience, and the ongoing struggle for representation and equality.

Talitha Agan

Keeping Biases and Stereotypes in Check: A Look at Native American Women in Women's History

In exploring Women's History, it's important to introduce an often-overlooked aspect of cultural awareness: the representation and perception of Native American women. This aspect sometimes goes unnoticed, yet it plays a crucial role in understanding the broader narrative. A journey through history must be undertaken with sensitivity and a deep understanding of the biases and stereotypes that have long obscured Native American cultures. The history taught to our parents and grandparents is laden with biases and stereotypes, and these continue to influence us today. It is crucial to acknowledge and become aware of how these perspectives have shaped our views in order to truly explore the vast and diverse stories of Women's History.

The Power of Images and Misrepresentation

From Victoria's Secret models donning headdresses on the runway to logos on products and cartoon characters, our society is saturated with images that depict Native American culture inappropriately. These portrayals often reduce a rich and diverse heritage to mere stereotypes, stripping away the complexity and dignity of Native American identities.

Susan Cabot in the 1951 film Tomahawk. She played a Cheyenne woman.

Cultural Appropriation: Understanding its Harm

"Cultural appropriation" describes when one cultural group adopts elements from another culture, often without proper context, leading to potential exploitation, mockery, or disrespect. This phenomenon dates back hundreds of years and has been particularly harmful to Native American communities, whose cultural symbols and artifacts are frequently misappropriated by mainstream culture. The Atlanta Braves' logo is of a tomahawk, and the "tomahawk chop" fan gesture continues to draw criticsm.

Native American culture is present everywhere in America, from the names of cities and rivers to the art and traditions that have been passed down through generations. Yet, the significance of these symbols and the people they represent are frequently overlooked and forgotten in mainstream society.

The Commercialization of Native American Imagery

Historically, Europeans quickly realized that "Indian" imagery was marketable, leading to the widespread commercialization of Native American representations. For example, the Land O'Lakes butter logo features a kneeling Native American woman, a symbol that commodifies and trivializes Native American identities for profit.

This trend permeates advertising. A glaring example is a chain of tanning salons in Alabama and Florida, which launched a Thanksgiving-themed ad campaign. The ad reads, "Have a Colorful Thanksgiving! The Indians brought more than just 'corn' to the first Thanksgiving... they brought Sexy Color!" This campaign was seen as offensive and displayed a significant level of ignorance to many individuals.

Disney's Characters: Tiger Lily and Pocahontas

The portrayal of Native American women in popular media has often perpetuated harmful stereotypes and misrepresentations. This is starkly evident in various forms of entertainment, most notably in animations and films. Cartoon characters serve as prime examples. While these characters might be intended to celebrate Native American culture, they frequently fall into the trap of oversimplification and cultural insensitivity, contributing to a skewed and incomplete understanding of Native American women's roles and identities.

Disney's portrayal of Native American culture has been highly problematic, particularly through characters like Tiger Lily from *Peter Pan* and Pocahontas. In *Peter Pan*, Tiger Lily is depicted as the daughter of a Native American chief, living in a stereotypical Native American village. The film's portrayal of Tiger Lily and her people is steeped in racist caricatures that mock and trivialize Native American cultures. The characters speak in broken English, wear exaggerated headdresses, and participate in wildly inaccurate representations of traditional ceremonies. This portrayal perpetuates damaging stereotypes and grossly misrepresents the richness and diversity of Native American cultures.

The character of Pocahontas, from the film Pocahontas, presents a different set of issues. While the film attempts to tell a more respectful story, it fails significantly in historical accuracy and realism. Pocahontas is depicted as a young adult woman, although in reality, she was around 12 years old when she encountered John Smith. This age disparity not only romanticizes a deeply problematic relationship but also distorts historical truths for the sake of creating a more palatable narrative for audiences. Furthermore, the film glosses over the complexities of Pocahontas's life and cultural heritage, presenting a simplified and sanitized version that benefits mainstream consumption while doing a disservice to her legacy and the true history of her people.

Both depictions have misled countless viewers, perpetuating harmful stereotypes and distorting the understanding of Native American cultures and histories. The enduring impact of these portrayals highlights the urgent need for more accurate and respectful representations in media.

Recognizing the Diversity Within Native American Cultures

One of the most important messages to convey is that Native Americans are not a monolith. The term "Native American" encompasses nearly 600 federally recognized tribes, each with its own unique traditions, languages, beliefs, and ways of life. Reducing Native American culture to a single category undermines the rich diversity of these communities.

The Significance of Regalia

Regalia, the sacred clothing, accessories, and artifacts worn by Native American individuals, is deeply symbolic and holds great significance. Each tribe has its own form of regalia, often handmade with meaningful colors and stitching. Wearing regalia is a form of self-expression and pride, reserved for powwows, ceremonies, and other important events.

The Offense of Costumes

In 2012, Victoria's Secret sparked controversy when American model Karlie Kloss (on right) walked the runway wearing a feathered headdress, a buckskin bikini, and turquoise jewelry. This outfit, intended to symbolize Thanksgiving, ignited outrage within the Native American community for its cultural misappropriation. Numerous instances of cultural misappropriation have continued to surface, further shining a spotlight on the persistent issue of disrespect towards Native American cultures.

The fashion label Dsquared2 faced backlash for their inappropriate use of Native American-inspired designs in their collection. The title of their collection, "DSquaw," was particularly offensive, as it used a derogatory term for Native American women. <u>Critics pointed out</u> that the brand failed to acknowledge the cultural significance of the patterns and symbols they used, treating sacred imagery as mere fashion trends.

Recent incidents involving influencers have sparked backlash on social media. Often, influencers post photos wearing Native American headdresses, claiming it's part of a "festival look." These actions pose a continuous struggle for Native American communities to safeguard their cultural heritage from commodification and trivialization.

Beyond fashion shows, offensive cultural appropriation is prevalent in Halloween costumes and sports mascots, often sexualizing and disrespecting Native American culture. Halloween costumes, in particular, frequently perpetuate harmful stereotypes and reduce rich, diverse cultures to mere caricatures. Many popular costumes, from Native American headdresses to "tribal" outfits, not only misrepresent and trivialize sacred symbols but also contribute to the ongoing marginalization of Native American communities. By donning these costumes, individuals are often unaware of the deep cultural significance and the painful history associated with these symbols, leading to an insidious form of disrespect that perpetuates ignorance and insensitivity.

Recognizing our own biases, whether conscious or unconscious, is crucial when studying Women's History and the significant roles Native American women have played. Before exploring the history and contributions of Native American women, it is vital to approach with an open mind and a commitment to cultural respect. We need to recognize the biases and prejudices embedded in historical accounts, mainstream culture, and even our own thoughts. Awareness of these influences is the first step toward truly understanding our history and how our interpretations of it continue to evolve.

NAVIGATING CHANGE: Native American Women and the Columbian Exchange

When Christopher Columbus landed on the Caribbean island of San Salvador in 1492, he set off a chain of events that would profoundly reshape the lives of Native American women and their communities. This arrival of Europeans marked the beginning of an era characterized by dramatic shifts in social structures, health, and day-to-day living for Native American populations. This article explores the diverse effects of European contact, with a particular emphasis on the Columbian exchange.

The European exploration and colonization of the Americas involved many nations, each driven by the desire to exploit the New World's vast resources and wealth. The Spanish, French, Portuguese, Swedish, Dutch, and English all sought riches in the form of gold, enslaved people, furs, timber, and other valuable commodities. By the early 17th century, these ambitions had given rise to several permanent colonial settlements.

The Spanish established St. Augustine in Florida in 1565 and Santa Fe in New Mexico in 1609. The French founded Quebec in 1608, while the English set up several notable settlements: Jamestown in 1607, Plymouth in 1620, and Massachusetts Bay in 1630. These colonies became hubs of trade, conflict, and cultural exchange, profoundly impacting the Native American populations they encountered.

Defining the Columbian Exchange

In 1972, historian Alfred Crosby introduced the concept of the Columbian exchange, which describes the extensive transfer of plants, animals, culture, human populations, technology, and ideas between the Americas, West Africa, and Europe following Columbus's voyages. This exchange had profound implications, particularly for Native American women. In a 2011 article in _Smithsonian Magazine_, Crosby wrote:

"Columbus brought them [New and Old worlds] together, and almost immediately and continually ever since, we have had an exchange of native plants, animals, and diseases moving back and forth across the oceans between the two worlds. A great deal of the economic, social, and political history of the world is involved in the exchange of living organisms between the two worlds."

 This ongoing exchange has significantly shaped global history. The arrival of cacao in the New World due to this exchange brought about a profound transformation in the way people across the globe experience daily life. This humble bean, which serves as the foundation of chocolate as we know it, has woven itself into the fabric of our existence, leaving an indelible mark on our modern world and shaping our cultural and culinary landscape in ways that continue to resonate today.

Impact on Native American Women's Lives

The Columbian Exchange introduced not only new crops and livestock but also invasive species and diseases. The arrival of Old-World animals and crops — such as cattle, pigs, sheep, rice, barley, and oats — significantly altered Native agricultural practices and diets. The horse, in particular, revolutionized Native American cultures, enhancing mobility, hunting practices, and spiritual life. While some of these changes offered benefits, they also disrupted traditional farming systems and caused environmental degradation.

The impact of these introductions profoundly affected the lives of Native women. Wheat and sugar, for example, became staple ingredients, changing traditional cooking methods and diets. However, the increased demand for farming these crops often placed additional labor burdens on women, who were typically responsible for food production and preparation.

European settlers' arrival also introduced manufactured goods like cloth and metalwork, which started to replace traditional tools and textiles. This shift had a ripple effect on gender roles, as women, who were often the primary weavers and artisans, sometimes found their skills less in demand. Additionally, the forced labor systems implemented by Europeans stripped many Native American women of their autonomy and subjected them to new forms of exploitation.

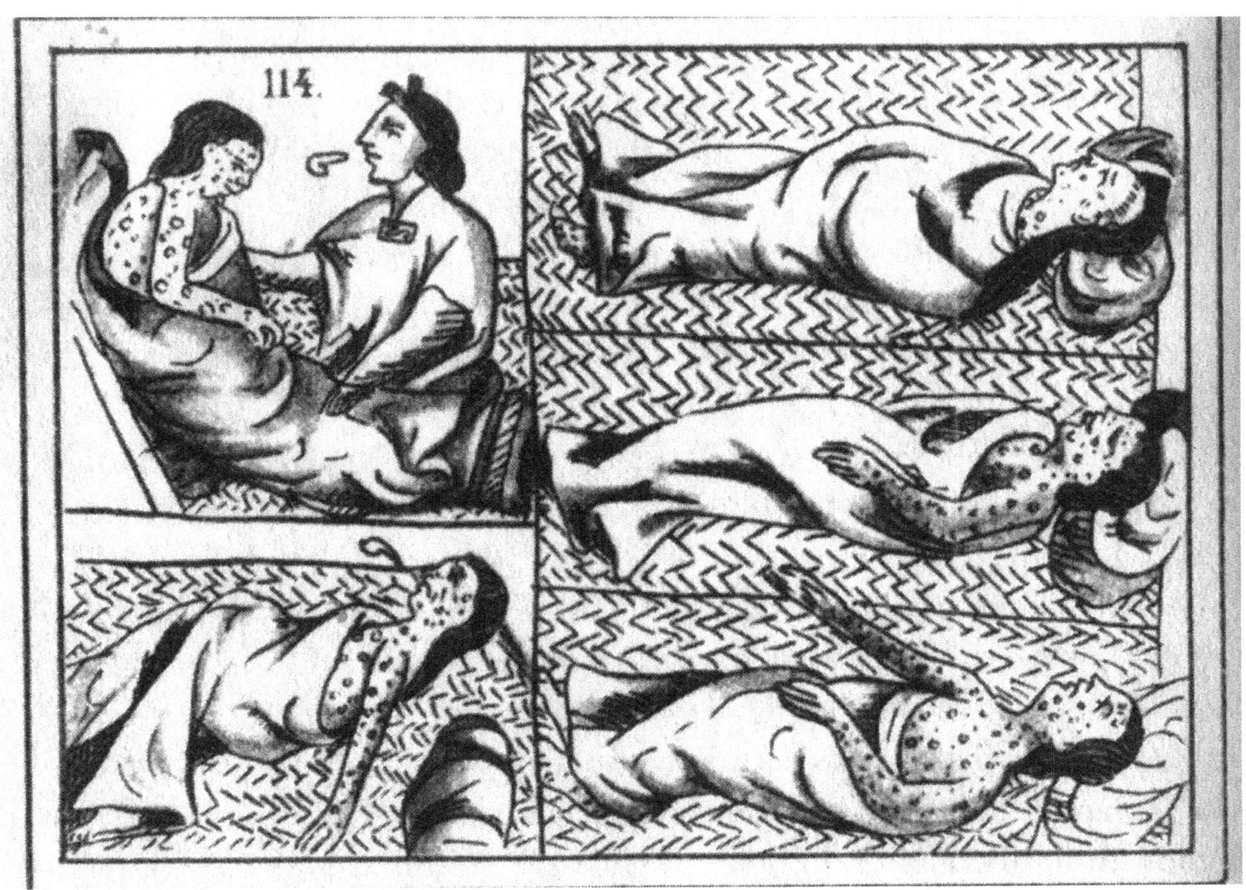

16th century Aztec drawing of smallpox victims. This smallpox epidemic struck the Aztec capital of Tenochtitlán in 1520 is taken from the Florentine Codex, a post conquest history written and illustrated by Aztec scribes.

The Devastating Impact of Virgin Soil Epidemics

Another critical but often devastating aspect of European contact and the Columbian exchange was the spread of infectious diseases, known as virgin-soil epidemics. These epidemics occurred when populations with no previous exposure to certain diseases encountered them for the first time, rendering them defenseless against the infections.

Health Effects and Community Roles

The introduction of diseases such as smallpox, measles, chickenpox, malaria, yellow fever, influenza, and even the common cold had catastrophic effects.

Historians estimate that between 1492 and 1800, over 70% of the native population was decimated due to these diseases.

For women, the health crises wrought by these epidemics were particularly severe. Many Native American communities were matrilineal, meaning descent and inheritance were traced through the mother. The loss of large numbers of women disrupted social structures, leading to a breakdown in community cohesion and continuity. Women who survived the epidemics often found themselves taking on additional roles, striving to maintain their families and cultural practices amidst a landscape of loss and upheaval.

Transformative Effects of European Trade and Settlements

Economic and Social Shifts

The establishment of European settlements like St. Augustine, Jamestown, and Quebec marked the beginning of permanent changes in the economic and social fabric of Native American life. Women were thrust into new economic systems that often devalued their traditional roles. Moreover, things like the fur trade changed patterns of land use and resource management, further altering women's roles within their communities.

Cultural Impacts

Cultural exchanges between Europeans and Native Americans were intricate and often biased towards European norms.

The above image titled "America" by Theodor Galle (circa 1580) vividly encapsulates this disparity. It depicts a fully clothed and armored European man, symbolizing Europe and its perceived civility. In stark contrast, an unclothed Native American woman represents America, reflecting the European view of Native Americans as uncivilized and naive. Additionally, the depiction of a human leg roasting on a fire alludes to the European belief in Native American cannibalism. Through allegory, Galle employs human figures to represent entire nations, highlighting the cultural imposition and skewed perceptions that accompanied European colonization.

Apsaroke woman on horseback, packhorse beside her. ca. 1908.

CONCLUSION

The arrival of Europeans dramatically altered the lives of Native American women and their communities. The Columbian exchange and virgin-soil epidemics introduced new goods and crops, reshaping traditional roles, disrupting social structures, and imposing new cultural norms. It's critical to examine how European contact affected the status of Native American women. Some historians assert that women lost their standing relative to men as colonizers imposed their gender norms on Native societies. Conversely, others argue that European traders and settlers provided women with new opportunities for political and economic leadership within their communities. These impacts likely varied across different Native American societies. Understanding these effects is essential for a comprehensive grasp of the historical experiences of Native American women during this transformative period.

Journeying Through the Lives of Pueblo Women in the Southwest from Pre-Contact to Colonization

On the housetop — Hopi. Arizona, ca. 1906.

The history of Native American women is a testament to resilience, strength, and cultural richness. The Pueblo, known for their unique adobe homes and intricate social structures, have a deep-rooted history that predates European contact by centuries. This article will touch on the pivotal roles of Pueblo women within their societies, exploring their cultural practices, religious beliefs, and the impact of Spanish colonization.

The Pueblo, residing in present-day Arizona, New Mexico, Colorado, and Utah, developed a highly organized society long before the Spanish arrived. Their name, "Pueblo," also refers to their distinctive multi-story adobe dwellings. By the time the Spanish encountered them in the mid-16th century, Pueblo societies were thriving, boasting a population of around 250,000 people living in over 100 towns and villages.

Matrilineal Kinship

One of the most notable aspects of traditional Pueblo society was its matrilineal kinship system. In Pueblo culture, lineage and inheritance were passed down through the female line. Children belonged to their mother's family, and family descent was traced through her. This matrilineal structure, practiced as far back as 600 A.D., placed women at the center of family and community life.

In Pueblo society, sons moved into their wives' households upon marriage, known as a matrilocal arrangement. Both men and women had the freedom to end marriages and choose new partners without social stigma. This practice reflected the belief that primary identity was derived from one's mother's lineage rather than marital ties. As a result, older women held significant influence within the community.

Hopi woman painting small pottery vessel. ca. 1906

Role of Pueblo Women

Agricultural Prowess

The Pueblo people, primarily agriculturalists, were adept farmers who sustained large populations in permanent villages despite the arid climate and minimal rainfall. Agriculture in the southwest north of Mexico reached its peak development, and by the 1500s, the Pueblos practiced intensive farming with crops introduced from Mexico, including maize (corn), beans, and squash — known as the Mesoamerican Triad. These domesticated crops provided complete protein and nutrition, enabling sizable populations to thrive. Although men were responsible for trade and defense, they also played a significant role in farming, particularly in tending to the corn crops. To support their agricultural practices, the Pueblo constructed irrigation canals, ensuring their success even in challenging conditions.

Pueblo Pottery and Population Growth

With the advent of agriculture came the need for durable storage and cooking vessels. Pueblo women became skilled potters, creating intricate and functional pottery. The creation of fired pottery marked a shift towards a more settled lifestyle, as the weight of these objects indicated less mobility.

These containers also allowed women to boil foods for long periods of time, including making cereal for children, thus reducing the duration of breastfeeding and increasing the chances of higher fertility. Thus, the advent of fired pottery was vital for food preparation and storage, contributing to increased fertility rates and population growth.

The mealing trough — Hopi, Pueblo. ca. 1906.

Grinding Tradition

Pueblo women played a crucial role in food preparation. They used traditional tools, such as manos and metates, to grind maize into meal and other materials into powder. This meticulous grinding process was not only essential for food production but also held spiritual significance, as women viewed their contributions as vital to their community's well-being.

The young Pueblo Hopi women in the photograph sport the unique tribal hairstyle known as squash blossom or butterfly whorls, characteristic of the Hopi. This intricate hairdo was created by winding the hair around a curved piece of wood to achieve a round shape, which was then removed. This elaborate style was reserved for unmarried young women.

Religious and Healing Practices

The traditional Pueblo had a rich religious life, with various societies responsible for weather, fertility, hunting, war, entertainment, and healing. Before Spanish contact, their religious practices were deeply interconnected with the supernatural and highly ritualized.

Healing Societies

Women healers played a significant role in curing ailments within their communities. Different societies helped in treating specific conditions. For instance, the Lakón society of the Hopi cured skin troubles using the plant katoki, while the Márawu society treated rheumatic fever with hovakpi. The methods often involved blowing crushed herbs onto the infection and then sucking out the disease, reflecting a deep connection between spiritual beliefs and healing practices.

Tablita woman dancer — San Ildefonso, Pueblo.
ca. 1905

The Impact of Spanish Contact

The arrival of the Spanish in the mid-16th century brought dramatic changes to Pueblo life. Led by Vasquez de Coronado in 1540, the Spaniards initially sought gold in the Southwest but left a trail of devastation when they found none. Subsequent expeditions in 1598 aimed at colonizing New Mexico imposed Spanish rule through force and suppressed traditional Pueblo culture. Additionally, Pueblo women suffered rape and sexual exploitation at the hands of Spanish soldiers. By 1609, the Spanish had established a foothold at Santa Fe.

Cultural Suppression

The Franciscan friars who accompanied the Spanish settlers and soldiers pressured the Pueblo to abandon their traditional religious practices in favor of Catholic Christian rites. This suppression profoundly affected Pueblo women, particularly those involved in fertility cults and rituals connected to sexuality and spirituality. The Church aimed to restructure the division of labor, imposing European gender roles and advocating for monogamous, lifelong marriages.

Resistance and Resilience

Despite the oppression, the Pueblo people resisted. In 1680, they united in the Pueblo Revolt, one of the most effective resistance movements in American history. This revolt successfully drove the Spanish out for 12 years, demonstrating the resilience and strength of the Pueblo communities.

The history of Pueblo women before Spanish contact is a story of strength, adaptability, and cultural significance. From their central roles in matrilineal kinship systems to their contributions as artisans and healers, Pueblo women were foundational to their communities. The resilience they displayed in the face of Spanish colonization underscores their enduring legacy.

Negotiating Power: The Influence of Native American Women in Fur Trading Roles in Early Northeastern America

The fur trade played a pivotal role in North American history, shaping the economic and social interactions between Native Americans and European traders. From the 16th century onward, this trade profoundly impacted the lives of Native American women, especially in the Northeast, where they were instrumental in providing and processing many of the traded items. This article explores how the fur trade influenced the cultural roles, social status, and daily lives of Native American women, with a particular focus on the Ojibwe in the Northeast.

The Cultural Significance of the Fur Trade

The fur trade, more than any other endeavor, significantly contributed to the European exploration and opening of the wilderness north of Mexico. It also facilitated extensive interactions between Europeans and Native Americans.

The colonial European powers of France, England, the Netherlands, Russia, and, to a lesser extent, Spain were all deeply involved in the extensive commercial exploitation of animal pelts and skins. The high demand for furs in Europe drove this trade, and from the 16th century to the mid-18th century, beaver pelts and deerskins were highly prized. By then, European hunters had nearly driven their own beaver and deer populations to extinction. In a continent known for its prolonged rainy and snowy winters, waterproof and warm clothing were essential. Felted beaver pelts met both of these needs. Moreover, they were very fashionable, with trends in fashion greatly influencing the fur trade.

Native Americans were knowledgeable hunters and suppliers of pelts, making them valuable trading partners, which exposed them to European culture. They traded their goods for European items, including practical tools like iron utensils and decorative items such as colorful cloth and beads. The diverse array of these European goods included cloth, blankets, utensils, tools, silver jewelry, thread, beads, and alcohol (and its detrimental effects). In exchange, these items were traded for furs, food (namely wild rice and maple sugar in the Northeast), and Native American-crafted supplies, such as canoes. In the Northeast, the French capitalized on the fur trade, with their involvement dating back to the 1530s.

Native American women, skilled in various crafts and crucial domestic tasks, emerged as indispensable partners in this fur trade exchange, including through marital alliances with the French traders. They integrated European products into their daily lives, using these new tools for activities like cooking. These trade goods not only provided material benefits but also elevated their status within their communities.

Native American Chippewa woman boiling syrup, probably maple syrup, on an open fire. ca. 1908-1912

The Northeast and the Ojibwe

During the fur trade, the Ojibwe (also known as the Chippewa, Anishinaabe, and sometimes Ojibwa) inhabited a varied environment within the Northeast cultural area. The Northeast extends along the coast to the Mississippi Valley and from the Great Lakes to the tidewater regions of present-day Virginia and North Carolina. In their forested area within this region, near the Great Lakes, their diet was sustained by a blend of hunting, gathering, fishing, and farming. They primarily lived in dome-shaped birchbark structures called wigwams and occasionally used tipi-shaped shelters.

The fur trade eventually had a profound impact on Ojibwe social and economic life, replacing traditional items with European goods and depleting natural resources. As territories expanded to access more fur-bearing animals, subsistence activities shifted towards trapping, with a focus on beaver and other valuable pelts. This shift led to a reduction in traditional hunting and fishing practices, which were previously central to their food supply. Increased dependence on European traders for essential goods created a precarious situation, raising concerns about potential starvation, especially during harsh winters or when fur-bearing animal populations declined. The long-term effects included environmental degradation and significant changes in Ojibwe culture and social structures.

Influence and Authority of Ojibwe Women

The fur trade was not confined to distant French forts; much of it took place within Ojibwe villages and nearby forts. This proximity allowed Ojibwe women to be more actively involved in trading activities. They were responsible for tanning and processing hides, traditionally from deer or moose, to create moccasins, leggings, breechcloths, and dresses. By processing the furs for trade, women had significant control over the materials and their distribution, further increasing their influence. Women also contributed to the economy by making clothing, tools, and other goods, such as birchbark canoes, that were exchanged in these trade networks. Their involvement extended beyond mere labor, as they played key roles in negotiating and maintaining trade relationships.

ca. 1850 lithograph shows Native American women harvesting rice in birchbark canoe, indicating that the women are probably Chippewa.

This integral participation not only bolstered their economic standing but also solidified their social and political influence within their communities. Ojibwe women played a crucial role in aiding French fur traders to adapt to their new surroundings, frequently through marriage alliances. They provided essential knowledge, skills, and labor, enabling traders to survive and thrive. Their contributions were fundamental to the success of the fur trade, highlighting their vital role in the economic and social fabric of their communities.

Strategic Marriages: Cementing Alliances and Trade Relations

Ojibwe marriages were characterized by the mutual decision of two individuals to share their lives, often marked by ceremonial gift exchanges. In traditional Ojibwe culture, honor and prestige were deeply tied to acts of generosity. Their society thrived on principles of reciprocity, where gift-giving played a pivotal social role. These ceremonial exchanges upheld kinship expectations and established reciprocal relationships of mutual support and obligation. This cultural practice extended to strategic partnerships between Ojibwe women and European fur traders, promoting mutual benefits and solidifying trade relationships.

The interaction between Ojibwe women and European, often French, traders led to significant cultural exchanges. For instance, French goods were quickly integrated into daily life and ceremonial practices. This exchange was not one-sided; Ojibwe knowledge, particularly that of women, was invaluable to these traders. Women taught them survival skills, including food preparation and clothing manufacture, which were vital for enduring the harsh climates of the Northeast.

From the Ojibwe perspective, these marriages were crucial for maintaining a consistent flow of goods. A French trader who married into the community was more likely to return, potentially offering greater generosity and more favorable trade deals. For fur traders, Ojibwe wives held significant social and economic value. Many prominent traders married the daughters of Ojibwe leaders, thereby securing influential allies among their Native American clients. These familial ties fostered strong alliances and facilitated smoother trade relations.

While some historians argue that these marriages commodified women, many believe that Native women embraced these alliances for their practical benefits. By enhancing communication, Native women frequently acted as interpreters and cultural mediators, significantly improving the flow of information and trade. Serving as crucial connectors between their communities and French traders, they shaped trade practices and enabled the exchange of information and goods.

Tshusick, an Ojibwa woman, dressed in red and black, wearing medals and holding a flower Coloured Lithograph 1837

The Trapper's Bride, 1845.
Alfred Jacob Miller

CONCLUSION

The fur trade brought profound changes to the lives of Native American women in the Northeast. By integrating European goods into their daily lives, they gained material advantages and elevated their social status. Their roles expanded beyond traditional boundaries, enabling them to exert significant influence over trade processes and community dynamics.

The resilience and adaptability of Native American women, who navigated the complexities of cultural exchange, contributed to the fur trade in ways that were not merely ancillary but central to its success.

Revisiting Women's History: Decoding Bias in Champlain's Accounts of Huron Society

This article explores how Champlain's European worldview influenced his depiction of Huron women, often resulting in a distorted understanding of their customs and way of life. It examines how his observations were filtered through the lens of European colonizing practices and beliefs. Recognizing these misrepresentations is essential for Women's History, as it underscores the importance of critically evaluating historical narratives. Many accounts of women's diverse experiences were documented by colonial oppressors, and it is these records that have shaped our perceptions of Native women over time.

In the early 17th century, French explorer Samuel de Champlain forged extensive trade alliances and documented his encounters with Native Americans. One notable account from 1616 details his interactions with the Huron people from the Northeast, including Huron women. While Champlain's observations offer valuable historical insights into the lives of these women, they are significantly influenced by his European biases and cultural context.

18th-century watercolor

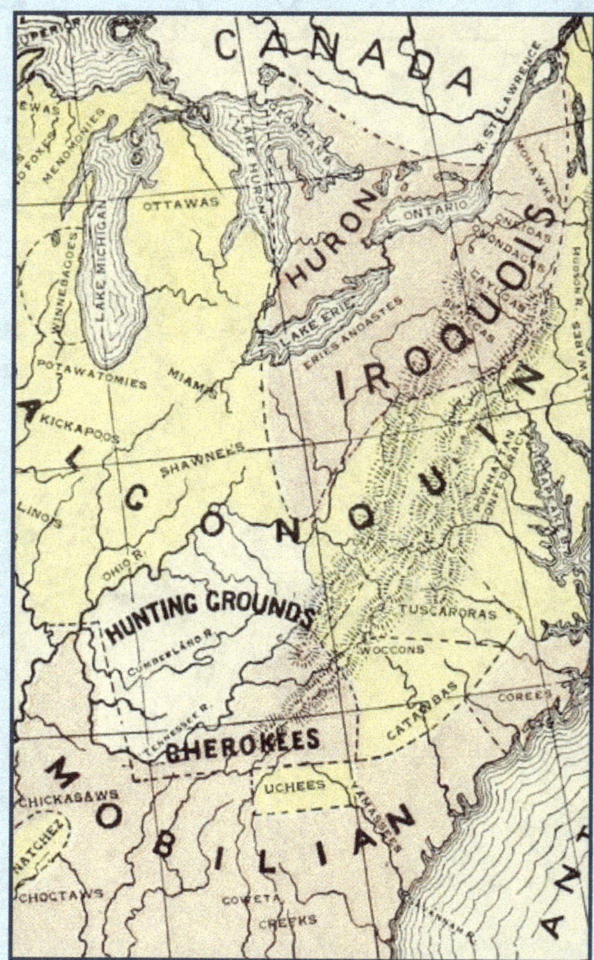

The Huron: Middlemen of the Great Lakes Trade Empire

The Huron, originally known as the Wyandot, are part of the Ontario Iroquoian-speaking groups inhabiting the Great Lakes region. The term "Huron" was coined by the French in the 17th century, derived from the Old French word "hure," referring to the distinctive bristly hairstyle of Huron men.

From 1616 to 1649, the Huron and their neighbors established a trade empire among Northeast Native Americans. They acted as middlemen by trading agricultural products for pelts, which they exchanged with the French in Quebec or Montreal. Skilled farmers, the Huron cultivated crops like corn, beans, squash, sunflowers, and tobacco. Women primarily managed farming, while men focused on hunting and managing tobacco plants.

Champlain: Architect of French-Native Relations and Conflict

Samuel de Champlain came from modest roots but became one of France's most noted explorers. He first arrived in North America in 1603 and helped found Quebec in 1608. Champlain's explorations included mapping areas of the northern Great Lakes and establishing trade agreements with various Native Americans. Champlain's successful trade alliances led to prosperity for the Quebec colony. However, his ties also led to conflicts, such as the 1609 battle where he helped the Huron fight the Iroquois, igniting 150 years of hostility between the Iroquois and the French.

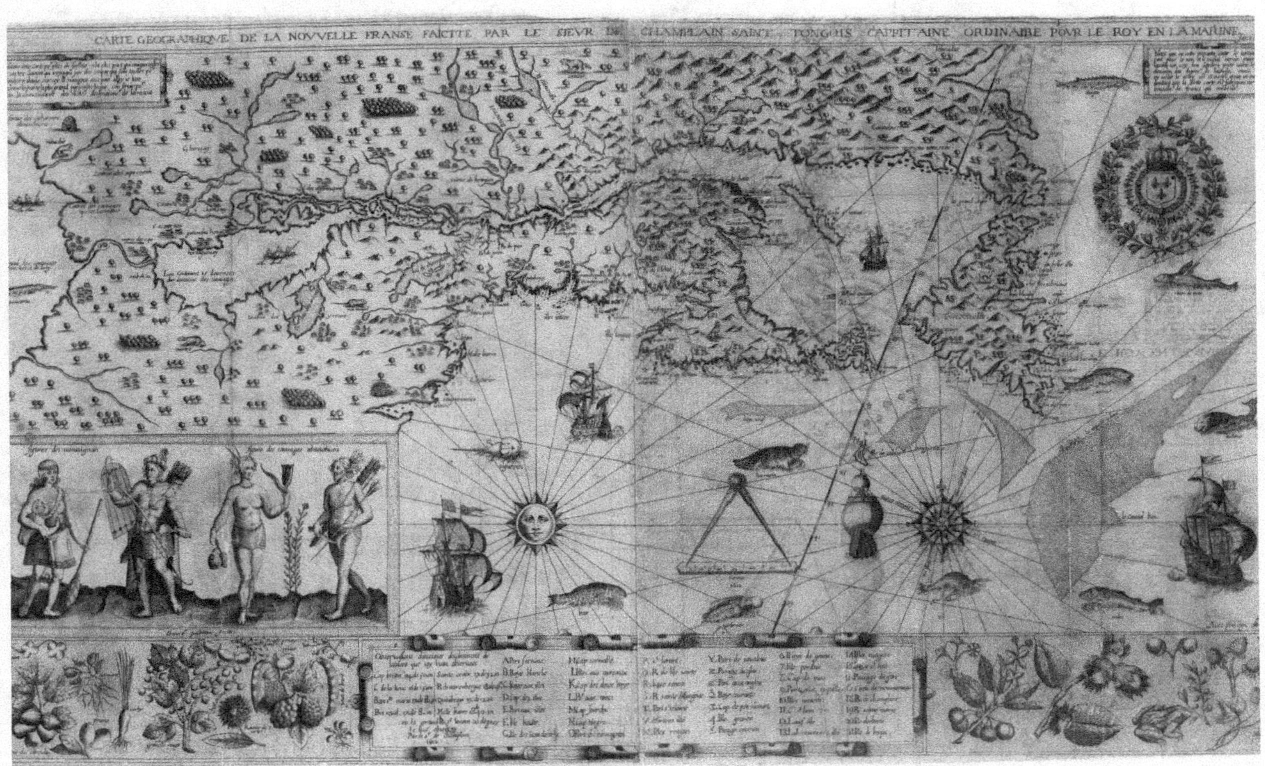

Map of New France drawn by explorer Samuel de Champlain in 1612.

1616 Huron Society Seen Through Champlain's European Eyes

To thoroughly examine Samuel de Champlain's observations of Huron society, his account will be presented section by section. Following the presentation of each section, an analysis will be provided, examining how Champlain's European biases and the context of European colonization influenced his portrayals, particularly regarding Huron women.

> These people are of a rather merry disposition, although there are many of them who have a gloomy and saturnine expression. They are well-formed and proportioned and body, some of the men being very strong and robust. And there are also women and girls who are very beautiful and attractive in figure, coloring (although it is olive) and in features, all in proportion; And their breasts hang down hardly at all, unless they are old. Some of them are very powerful and of extraordinary height. They have almost all the care of the house and the work; for they till the ground, plant the Indian corn, lay up wood for winter, beat the hemp and spin it, make fishing-nets from the thread, catch fish, and do other necessary things. They also harvest their corn, store it, prepare it to eat, and attend to their household affairs.

Champlain's initial observations reveal a mix of admiration and condescension. He notes the physical attributes of the Huron people, describing them as well-formed and proportioned. His remarks, filtered through a European lens, blend praise with critique. Champlain, for example, characterizes Huron women as beautiful, yet adds the caveat "although it is olive," which underscores a Eurocentric beauty standard that implicitly contrasts them with European, light-skinned women. His focus on attributes like breast firmness further underscores a superficial judgment based on European ideals.

Champlain also observes that Huron women are primarily responsible for domestic and agricultural labor. While this highlights the gender roles within Huron society, his framing implies subservience, reflecting European gender norms of the time. Phrases like "serve as mules," used to describe women carrying baggage for their husbands, further emphasize his biased perspective, portraying Huron women as overburdened and oppressed.

Champlain's depiction of gender roles within Huron society further reveals a bias toward European norms. He notes that while women handle most domestic and agricultural tasks, men hunt and go to war. His characterization of men as idle once their tasks are complete contrasts sharply with his depiction of hardworking women, suggesting an imbalance that may not accurately reflect Huron values. Champlain's limited understanding of the Huron's complex social dynamics is evident in his failure to recognize the value of all contributions.

Champlain's criticism of Huron men for perceived laziness fails to recognize the importance of communal activities and leisure in promoting social cohesion and mental well-being, especially considering the demands of their daily tasks. Additionally, his portrayal of men as merely doing "nothing but hunt for deer and other animals, catch fish, make cabins and go to war" overlooks the complexities and interdependencies inherent in these roles. Each task requires significant effort and time — hunting demands not only skill but also a deep understanding of the land and animal behavior, while fishing requires patience and knowledge of various techniques. Constructing cabins is a labor-intensive endeavor that takes considerable time and craftsmanship, and engaging in warfare involves preparation and strategy amid inherent dangers. By oversimplifying these roles, Champlain neglects the dedication and multifaceted nature of their work.

Champlain's descriptions are likely influenced by European (colonizer) biases, leading to misunderstandings of the cultural significance of social and ceremonial practices among Native Americans, particularly the Huron. His European perspective fails to grasp the intricacies of Huron social structures and the importance of communal activities within their society.

They have a sort of marriage among them, which is like this: when a girl is 11, 12, 13, 14 or 15 years old, she will have several suitors, according to her good graces, who will woo her and ask the consent of her father and her mother, although often the girls do not accept their consent. Those who are the best and most discreet submit to their wishes. This lover, or suitor, gives the girl some necklaces, chains and bracelets of wampum. If the girl finds the suitor agreeable, she accepts this present. This done, he comes to sleep with her three or four nights without saying a word, when they gather the fruit of their affections. And it often happens that after having spent a week or a fortnight together, if they cannot agree, she will quit her suitor, who forfeits his necklaces and other gifts made by him. Frustrated in his hope, he will seek another woman, and she another suitor; and thus they continue until a satisfactory union is made.

There are many girls who pass their entire youth thus was several husbands, who are not alone in the enjoyment of the creature, married though they are; for, when night comes, the young women run from one cabin to another, as do the young men, on their part, visiting any girls they please. They do so without violence, however, referring the whole matter to the wish of the woman. The husband will do the same thing to a woman neighbor, without there being any jealousy among them on that account, or, and any case, very little; and they incur no ill-repute or insult for it, for it is the custom of the country.

In this section, Champlain provides a detailed account of Huron marriage customs, emphasizing the freedom women had in choosing their partners. He describes a practice where young women could have multiple suitors and even leave a suitor if they were not compatible. Champlain is somewhat scandalized by this, as it contrasts sharply with European norms of monogamous, lifelong marriages. His account highlights the agency Huron women had in their relationships, which was unusual by European standards. However, his tone suggests a judgmental perspective, viewing their customs as promiscuous and lacking moral discipline, failing to consider the cultural context in which these practices were normal and acceptable.

The Huron social structure allowed for personal autonomy and choice, particularly for women. The flexibility in relationships and the ability to choose partners based on mutual consent rather than rigid societal expectations provided a form of social stability and personal freedom that Champlain may have overlooked. His remarks reveal his cultural biases, describing Huron customs as informal and temporary compared to European marriage standards.

In contrast, 17th-century European marital norms were often characterized by strict adherence to societal expectations, with marriages frequently arranged for economic or social gain rather than love or personal choice. Women in Europe were typically expected to conform to the role of submissive wives, with limited agency in selecting their partners. These unions were often marked by a sense of permanence and legal binding, resulting in a clear delineation of roles within the household. Unlike the Huron, where women had the freedom to choose multiple partners and where relationships could evolve, European marriages were often rigid and hierarchical, reinforcing male authority.

Champlain's focus on the lack of permanent unions among the Huron and the freedom of women to choose multiple partners reflects his inability to appreciate the Huron's distinct social norms. He viewed their practices as less legitimate or civilized, failing to recognize that the Huron's flexible and consensual approach to relationships might offer a different kind of stability and satisfaction. The contrast between Huron and European marital practices highlights significant cultural differences, emphasizing how societal values shape personal relationships and norms surrounding marriage in different contexts.

> When the women have children, the preceding husbands return to them, to show them the friendship and affection that they had borne them in the past, saying that it is more than that of any other man, and that the child who is to be born is his and of his begetting. Another will tell her the same thing; and so it is at the choice and option of the woman to take and accept him who pleases her most. Having gained by her loves a great deal of wampum, she remains with him without leaving him anymore; or, if she leaves him, it must be for some important reason, other than impotence, for he is on trial. Nevertheless, while she is with her husband she does not cease to indulge herself freely; yet she keeps herself at home and busy always with the household, making a good appearance.

Champlain noted that Huron children often faced uncertainties regarding their paternity, which led to property inheritance through the maternal line. This matrilineal system ensured that assets remained within the family, as the maternal lineage was clear. His observations reflected a social structure that diverged significantly from European patrilineal norms. However, Champlain's focus on paternity uncertainty revealed a bias toward European ideals of legitimacy and inheritance, limiting his understanding of the effectiveness and stability of the Huron system.

Matrilineal kinship, as seen in Huron society, empowers women by placing them at the center of familial structures. In these societies, lineage and inheritance follow the mother, granting women significant autonomy and enhancing their social status.

 As respected custodians of lineage, women enjoy greater control over resources and a stronger voice in decision-making, which fosters community support and maintains strong familial bonds, in stark contrast to the marginalization often experienced in patrilineal systems.

In 17th-century European societies, lineage and inheritance were primarily traced through men, placing women in subordinate roles and limiting their agency. Women were often expected to be obedient wives, reliant on husbands for economic stability, which stifled their personal freedoms and decision-making power. This rigid structure created significant barriers for women in accessing power and property, contrasting sharply with the freedoms Huron women enjoyed in choosing partners and influencing their families.

In light of these comparisons, one might argue that Champlain's perspective on Huron customs overlooked a more complex and functional social structure, in which women held substantial agency and respect, thereby casting doubt on the civility of his own European society.

Samuel de Champlain's observations of Huron society offer valuable historical insights but must be approached with a critical eye, given the biases inherent in his European perspective. Such early primary sources, viewed through the eyes of the colonizer, significantly influence our understanding of the roles of Native American women in history. While he documented various aspects of Huron life, his judgments were often filtered through his own colonial framework.

Iroquois Indians, United States ca. 1914

Iroquois Matriarchy: The Pinnacle of Female Political Power

In a world often dominated by patriarchal systems, the Iroquois, also known as the Haudenosaunee, stand out as a remarkable example of female political power and influence. Situated in the forests of present-day New York State and Ontario, Canada, the Iroquois nations — including the Mohawk, Oneida, Onondaga, Cayuga, and Seneca tribes — celebrated a societal structure where women thrived and wielded significant authority in governance, economy, and community wellbeing. This article explores the considerable influence of Iroquois women, emphasizing their distinctive roles and the lasting legacy they have imparted on views of gender roles and leadership, including their impact on the suffrage movement.

People of the Long House: The Birth of a Lasting Democracy in History

The Iroquois Confederacy, referred to as the League of Five Nations by the English and known as the Haudenosaunee Confederacy — meaning "People of the Long House" — was an intricate alliance of tribes. Some argue that the Iroquois Confederacy was established around 1650 in response to European colonization; however, the exact date when the nations united remains unknown. It is believed that this alliance has roots that extend back to time immemorial, making it one of the earliest and longest-lasting participatory democracies in the world. Today, the <u>Confederacy comprises six nations</u>, including the Tuscarora, alongside the original five.

In contrast to other Native American groups that tended to be more nomadic and decentralized, the Haudenosaunee established permanent villages and formulated a sophisticated political system. This system included a council of elders, where representatives from each tribe collaborated to make decisions collectively. The confederacy was founded by the prophet known as the Peacemaker, with the help of Aionwatha, more commonly recognized as Hiawatha.

While men participated in these councils, the power dynamics were far from male-dominated. Elder women of the clans, known as Clan Mothers, held vital roles in selecting and removing village chiefs. Each nation maintained its own council of chiefs, with selections made by these influential Clan Mothers, ensuring their significant impact on governance.

Iroquois Matrilineal Strength

Iroquois society was both matrilineal and matrilocal, meaning lineage is traced through the mother's line, and married couples typically lived with the wife's family. This societal structure placed women at the center of family and community life. It was common for Iroquois men to move into their wives' residences after marriage, ensuring that women maintained control over domestic and agricultural resources. Iroquois women were not just homemakers; they played a crucial role as the backbone of the village economy and governance.

Iroquois women held more formal power than the <u>matrilineal Pueblo</u> women. However, compared to European communities, where married women faced restrictions and severe penalties for adultery, both Pueblo and Iroquois women enjoyed greater freedom. These native marriages were often easily dissolved, allowing women to leave unhappy relationships with relative ease.

George Catlin, Chée-ah-ká-tchée, Wife of Nót-to-way, 1835–1836

Scenes about an Iroquois bark house, from a drawing by Jesse Cornplanter, a Seneca youth. Note the manner in whic[h] the corn braids are placed on the drying pole.

The Role of Iroquois Women in Village Life

Iroquois women played a central role in village life. While men cleared fields for planting, their primary responsibilities took them into the forests for hunting, trading, and warring with hostile tribes. Women, on the other hand, focused on village activities. They cultivated crops like corn, beans, and squash, gathered a variety of wild foods, prepared meals, distributed the bounty from hunting, and crafted baskets, pottery, and tools. Ultimately, they operated within a communal framework.

Inside the Longhouse — Iroquoian Village, Ontario, Canada. The 15th century Iroquoian Village was reconstructed on its original site.

The longhouses where they spent most of the year featured doors at both ends, lacked windows, and had smoke holes in the roof. Covered with bark, these structures featured benches along the walls for sleeping and storage. They were occupied from fall through spring, with less permanent dwellings utilized during more mobile seasons. These longhouses accommodated multiple families or extended families, with living areas partitioned and two families sharing a hearth. As families grew, so did the longhouses. Inside, women cooked and created crafts. This communal labor fostered a strong sense of unity and interdependence among the women, reinforcing their crucial role in society.

The Multifaceted Power of Iroquois Women

As stated, Clan Mothers played a significant role in political leadership, selecting male chiefs for the village and possessing the authority to depose them if they failed in their duties. This system ensured that male leaders remained accountable to the women who chose them, creating a balance of power that reinforced the importance of women within the governance structure of the community.

In addition to their political influence, women also controlled the food supply, managing both current crops and preserved food. Their authority extended to provisioning warriors and determining plans for raids and warfare. By controlling the distribution of food, women held a form of economic power that influenced every aspect of Iroquois life, including politics and social structures, thereby playing a crucial role in the community's overall stability and well-being.

Furthermore, women had a significant social and cultural influence, as they determined adoptions into the tribe, integrating captives, and minimizing losses due to disease and warfare. They could also call for the avenging of deaths within their families, which involved initiating raids and warfare. This dual role in nurturing community ties and protecting their families solidified their central position in Iroquois society, highlighting the multifaceted contributions of women to their culture.

Lafitau's Lens: Iroquois Women Through a Jesuit's Eyes

Joseph-Francois Lafitau, a Jesuit missionary in the early 18th century, provided a vivid depiction of Iroquois women in his work, "Moeurs des Sauvages Amériquains" (1734). His illustration of Canadian Iroquois women making maple sugar highlights their industrious nature and their roles in both agricultural and domestic tasks.

According to Lafitau:

Lafitau highlights the significant role women played in controlling land, which is crucial for understanding the social dynamics of their communities. His description emphasizes not only the communal and cooperative nature of their work but also illustrates how this control over essential resources empowered women and influenced societal structures. By managing land and resources, women contributed to the stability and sustainability of their communities, nurturing collaboration and shared responsibility. This aspect of their agency is vital, as it challenges traditional narratives that often overlook the contributions of women in historical contexts.

The Haudenosaunee Legacy: Fueling the Fight for Suffrage

The decisions of the Haudenosaunee Confederacy persist to this day, exemplifying a pure democracy that is the oldest continuously functioning system in the world. Even now, leadership responsibilities are shared between the Chief and the Clan Mother, reflecting a commitment to consensus.

Renowned suffrage leader Matilda Joslyn Gage once wrote of the Haudenosaunee, "Never was justice more perfect; never was civilization higher." Gage, alongside her contemporaries Elizabeth Cady Stanton and Susan B. Anthony, found inspiration in the Iroquois Confederacy, where women enjoyed substantial political power. This powerful example motivated their pursuit of women's rights in the United States.

By the 1880s, Gage and Stanton had dedicated decades to advancing women's rights but grew frustrated with the slow progress within their own society. American women of this era experienced severe legal and social subjugation, and U.S. common law rendered married women legally invisible. They had no rights to their property or bodies, and husbands could legally rape and beat their wives without inflicting permanent injury. Married women lost ownership of any property or income to their husbands, and children belonged solely to the father. Women were barred from voting, serving on juries, or acting as legal entities. In their search for a model of gender equality, Gage and Stanton turned to their neighbors — the Haudenosaunee.

The Haudenosaunee women's model of rights and governance provided suffragists with a vision of gender equality. For years, women had been told that their subjugation was divinely ordained and biologically determined. Seeing Native women who farmed, held political power, and lived in equality with men debunked these myths. Gage and Stanton shared their admiration for Haudenosaunee women through articles and speeches, highlighting their superior social, economic, and political structures.

Today, the legacy of Iroquois women's political power continues to influence discussions on gender and leadership. <u>The Six Nations clan mothers still nominate</u>, hold office, and remove their chiefs, demonstrating a long-standing tradition of female authority.

The story of Iroquois women and their impact on the suffrage movement underscores the importance of diverse perspectives in shaping a more equitable society. By looking beyond their own restrictive culture, suffragists found inspiration and a blueprint for gender equality among the Haudenosaunee, contributing to the broader fight for women's rights.

Overall, the narrative of Iroquois women is a testament to resilience, strength, and profound influence that have significantly shaped history. Their political authority, economic stewardship, and social leadership distinguished them from their European counterparts, enabling them to challenge conventional gender norms and play an influential role in the women's rights movement.

The Real Pocahontas: Untangling Disney Myths, History, and Modern Native Women's Issues

Throughout history, few figures have been as mythologized as Pocahontas. Her narrative has been told and retold, often with varying degrees of accuracy and romanticism, most notably in the iconic 1995 Disney animated film. While this film introduced her story to a new generation, it blurred the lines between fact and fiction. Beneath the romanticized Disney portrayal lies an intricate narrative that includes themes of cultural conflict, colonization, and power dynamics. This article seeks to untangle the myths from reality and explore why her story remains relevant today. Pocahontas's life offers valuable insights into the complexities of cultural interaction, identity, and representation, and it holds great significance within the framework of Women's History.

Pictured above is a Pocahontas stamp from 1907.

Disney's Pocahontas: A Tale of Love and Fiction

The 1995 Disney film "Pocahontas" brought her story to the big screen, making history as the first Disney movie to feature an adult female protagonist and a woman of color. It represented Disney's effort to engage with real historical events.

In introducing Pocahontas to a new generation, the film marked several significant milestones. It centered on an adult female lead and portrayed a real historical figure, presenting Pocahontas as an independent and fearless heroine with a strong sense of identity — traits that resonate with modern feminist ideals.

The strong and independent Pocahontas maintains a deep connection to nature throughout the animated film. Her relationship with John Smith is a central theme, framed as a love story that transcends cultural boundaries. However, the film takes creative liberties, portraying Pocahontas and Smith as adults falling in love despite the conflicts between their people.

Beyond the Screen: Historical Realities

Born in the 1590s as Matoaka, she was affectionately known as Pocahontas, meaning "full of mischief and joy." As the daughter of Chief Powhatan, the powerful leader of a large confederacy of tribes in Virginia's Tidewater region, her legacy is deeply embedded in history. Pocahontas was not an ordinary child; despite her father's many wives and children, she was seen as his favorite and often served as an advisor, even at a young age. The Powhatan people practiced agriculture, growing crops like corn, pumpkins, and beans, and their lives were rich in rituals. Growing up in a matrilineal society, where lineage and inheritance were traced through the mother, greatly influenced her role and status within the community.

In May 1607, the arrival of English colonizers marked a turning point for Pocahontas and American colonial history. This first successful English colony, following the failed Roanoke attempt, saw the arrival of John Smith, a 27-year-old war veteran with a tumultuous past.

The early days of Jamestown were marked by hardship and starvation, with some accounts suggesting that the <u>settlers resorted to cannibalism</u>. Tensions also ran high between the settlers and the native Powhatans. Amidst this turmoil, Pocahontas emerged as a key cultural mediator and diplomat. She frequently visited Jamestown, bridging her people and the English, often bringing much-needed food and supplies to the struggling colonists. Pocahontas significantly contributed to reducing tensions and promoting cooperation, frequently persuading her father, the Chief, to embrace a more conciliatory stance toward the English.

Rescue or Ritual? The Pocahontas-Smith Saga

One of the most debated events in Pocahontas's life is her alleged saving of John Smith. Her interaction with Smith has become legendary; following his capture by the Powhatan, it is said that she saved his life. This event and its account continue to be a topic of historical debate. According to Smith's account, she threw herself over him to prevent his execution by her tribe. In Smith's 1624 account, it states of the event:

"Two great stones were brought before Powhatan; then as many as could laid hands on him, dragged him to them, and thereon laid his head, and being ready with their clubs, to beate out his braines, Pocahontas the Kings dearest daughter, when no intreaty could prevaile, got his head in her armes, and laid her owne upon his to save hime from death."

Some historians, however, suggest that this event may have been a misunderstood adoption ceremony — a ritual designed to symbolize Smith's acceptance into the Powhatan tribe. This ceremony likely held significant cultural importance, as it represented not just a personal bond but also a strategic alliance between Smith and the Powhatans. As a matrilineal society, Powhatan women often held the ultimate authority in decision-making, influencing everything from daily life to broader political matters. In this context, the role of women — particularly Pocahontas, the Chief's favored daughter — in these ceremonies and their influence on tribal dynamics was essential, underscoring the complexity and richness of Powhatan society.

Pocahontas continued to visit Jamestown, acting as an intermediary between the settlers and her people. She even learned some English from John Smith. However, after Smith returned to England in 1609, tensions between the Powhatan and the settlers escalated.

Sandstone 1825 Capitol Rotunda

Kidnapping and Marriage to John Rolfe

In 1613, Pocahontas was kidnapped by the English during hostilities between the two groups. During her captivity, she converted to Christianity and took the baptized name Rebecca.

She later married John Rolfe, a tobacco planter ten years her senior, in 1614, which helped establish a period of relative peace between the settlers and the Powhatan. While the English often employed a strategy of exclusion in their colonial expansion, particularly towards Native Americans, the marriage in question exemplified a practice of inclusion. This approach was more commonly embraced by the French and Spanish during their colonial endeavors.

Baptism of Pocahontas on top, a 1624 engraving of the abduction of Pocahontas in the middle, and a print showing the wedding of Pocahontas and John Rolfe at bottom.

Journey to England

In 1616, Pocahontas traveled to England with her husband and their son, Thomas. Her presence was intended to showcase the success of English colonization and the potential for harmonious relations with Native Americans. It also promoted the Virginia Company's efforts to attract more settlers and investors. Her presence in London was a sensation; she was presented to English society as an example of the "civilized savage," even meeting Queen Anne. However, the trip also exposed her to the stark realities of English power and the vast differences between her homeland and the colonizers' society.

Tragically, as she prepared to return to Virginia in 1617, Pocahontas fell ill and died at around 21 years of age, probably from pneumonia or tuberculosis. She was buried in St. George's Church in Gravesend, England, far from her homeland.

Separating History from Hollywood

While the Disney movie captures the essence of Pocahontas's character — her bravery, curiosity, and desire for peace — it diverges significantly from historical accuracy. The real Pocahontas was only around 10 or 11 years old when she met John Smith, who was nearly three times her age. Their relationship was not romantic; rather, Pocahontas's interactions with the settlers were focused on diplomacy and survival.

The enduring love story between Pocahontas and John Smith persists largely because it appeals to Western sensibilities. It presents a "good Indian" narrative, where Pocahontas embraces Christianity and Western culture, offering a comforting storyline that downplays the colonial exploitation of Native Americans.

Disney was not the first to creatively reinterpret the relationship between Smith and Pocahontas; many accounts exist, including the 1953 United Artists film "Captain John Smith and Pocahontas," directed by Lew Landers.

The Influence of Disney's Pocahontas

Disney's "Pocahontas" received mixed reviews upon its release, praised for its breathtaking animation and unforgettable music, yet criticized for historical inaccuracies and inconsistent storytelling. Despite these flaws, the film made a significant impact, particularly through its portrayal of a strong, empowered female lead. Pocahontas marked a shift away from traditional Disney princesses, presenting a brave and self-reliant heroine.

Critics have noted that Pocahontas's character laid the foundation for later Disney heroines like Mulan and Moana, who embody themes of independence and courage. However, the film also perpetuates certain stereotypes and oversimplifies the complexities of Pocahontas's life. It offers an idealized vision of cultural harmony, glossing over the more troubling realities of colonialism. The film simplifies the political dynamics between the Powhatan and the English, prioritizing a romanticized narrative over the broader context of colonization and conflict.

For many Native Americans, the depiction of Pocahontas as a "good Indian" who admired and assimilated into English culture is problematic, as it neglects the resistance and resilience of Indigenous peoples. This portrayal has historically allowed those in white American culture to feel good about their past, suggesting that colonization was beneficial and welcomed by some Native Americans. Additionally, the "good Indian" narrative conveniently absolves colonial powers of their transgressions against Indigenous peoples.

Pocahontas in Modern Context

Pocahontas's story remains profoundly relevant today, shedding light on cultural identity, representation, and the enduring legacies of colonialism. Her life also underscores the plight of <u>Missing and Murdered Indigenous Women (MMIW)</u>, a tragic issue that persists. Pocahontas can be viewed as one of the earliest and most notable victims of this ongoing crisis.

The epidemic of MMIW has garnered heightened attention in recent years, yet it remains largely shrouded in silence. This unsettling crisis reflects deep-seated systemic racism and historical injustices that persist in our society. Indigenous women face disproportionately high rates of violence and homicide, with the <u>murder rate being ten times higher</u> than the national average for women living on reservations. Murder is the third leading cause of death for Native women, often exacerbated by factors such as poverty, inadequate access to resources, and failures within the justice system.

Pocahontas's abduction and forced assimilation into English society resonate with the experiences of many Indigenous women, especially in light of the tragic legacy of <u>Native American Boarding Schools</u>. Between 1819 and the 1970s, hundreds of thousands of Native American children were forcibly taken from their homes and families and placed in boarding schools run and/or supported by the federal government.

Her life, marked by both agency and vulnerability, encapsulates the broader historical narrative of Native American women.

Activist action made at Pocahontas' memorial in St. George's Church, Gravesend, Kent, England, where her body is buried. The statue was covered with a black cloth, the official plaque was replaced for a new one, a pile of soil was placed in front of the statue and a fabric was extended on the ground which read 'LET'S BRING HER BACK HOME'. The activists demand Matoaka's body to be sent back to the land she came from (current Virginia, US) as they understand that her memorial in England is a symbol of colonial power that perpetuates the abusive treatment of the Native American nations. 2015.

CONCLUSION

Pocahontas's life was a remarkable blend of cultural diplomacy and personal tragedy. While the Disney film has perpetuated certain myths, it has also kept her story alive in popular culture. Understanding the real Pocahontas allows us to appreciate her role as a bridge between two worlds and the complexities of early American history, and the profound impact of colonization on Native American women and their communities. By examining the fictionalized narratives alongside the historical truths of Pocahontas, we not only honor her legacy but also shed light on the significance of Missing and Murdered Indigenous Women (MMIW) and the ongoing investigations into Native American Boarding Schools.

CONCLUSION

In conclusion, this exploration of the experiences and contributions of Native American women underscores the vital role they played in shaping early North American history. From their involvement in the fur trade to their leadership within matrilineal societies, Indigenous women's stories reveal the strength and resilience inherent in their cultures. By challenging the stereotypes and misconceptions that have long overshadowed their narratives, we gain a deeper appreciation of their agency and the unique cultural heritage they represent.

Reflecting on the previous articles, consider how the complexities of Native American women's lives intersect with broader themes of identity, resistance, and empowerment. Each chapter not only highlights individual stories but also emphasizes the collective impact Indigenous women had in navigating the challenges posed by European contact and colonization

This examination serves as a reminder of the rich history that has shaped the United States, one that often overlooks the crucial contributions of Indigenous peoples.

I hope this book builds a deeper appreciation for the contributions of early Native American women to Women's History. Understanding this foundational history assists in connecting with contemporary issues, such as the urgent crisis of Missing and Murdered Indigenous Women (MMIW) and the ongoing inquiries into Native American Boarding Schools.

After all, the stories of Native American women are not just echoes of the past; they are powerful testimonies that continue to inspire resilience and underscore the importance of recognition, respect, and representation in our shared history.

Suggested Reading

INDIGENOUS AMERICAN WOMEN: DECOLONIZATION, EMPOWERMENT, ACTIVISM BY DEVON ABBOTT MIHESUAH

Book Overview

Devon Abbott Mihesuah offers a comprehensive examination of the evolving identities and roles of Indigenous women in America. Mihesuah, an Oklahoma Choctaw scholar, delves into how these women have been perceived and depicted by both non-Natives and themselves. The book highlights the pervasive impact of colonialism and patriarchal ideologies on Native women's traditional roles and their participation in academia. Mihesuah also explores the effects of Christianity and Euro-American ideologies on the relationships between Indigenous men and women, noting the escalation of sexism and violence against Indigenous women, as well as economic disparities and intratribal factionalism.

In the latter part of the book, Mihesuah focuses on the empowerment of modern Indigenous women, whether tribally, nationally, or academically. She sheds light on the often-overlooked contributions of Native women to the Red Power movement and discusses the distinctions between Native women who identify as feminists and those who see themselves as activists. Through a series of essays, Mihesuah provides a nuanced understanding of the challenges and triumphs faced by Indigenous women, making a compelling case for their critical role in both historical and contemporary contexts.

Why This Matters

This book is a pivotal work in the field of Women's History as it addresses the intersectionality of gender, race, and colonialism. Mihesuah's analysis brings to light the unique struggles and resilience of Indigenous women, who have often been marginalized in both mainstream feminist discourse and historical narratives. By documenting their experiences and contributions, the book not only fills a significant gap in historical scholarship but also challenges and expands the boundaries of Women's History.

Key Quotes

"Reconstructions of the intricacies of Indigenous women's lives must be specific to time and place, for tribal values, gender roles, appearances, and definitions of Native identity have not been static" (xv).

"Native women have been portrayed as everything from ugly squaws to beautiful princesses to New Age gurus. Many scholars argue that the 'Native-woman-as-princess is a compliment, but this distortion of reality is quite damaging" (36).

Book Details

Title: Indigenous American Women: Decolonization, Empowerment, Activism
Author: Devon Abbott Mihesuah
Publisher: University of Nebraska Press
Date: 2003

IMAGE CITATIONS

Not all images are included in the citations.

Introduction

- Curtis, Edward S, photographer. Offering the Pipe. , 1908. Photograph. https://www.loc.gov/item/2023635102/.

Keeping Biases and Stereotypes in Check: A Look at Native American Women in Women's History

- Atlanta Braves logo. By Extracted from a PDF file on the MLB website by Kalel2007 (talk), Fair use, https://en.wikipedia.org/w/index.php?curid=22426803

- Land O'Lakes. By Dustinlongstreth4real — Own work, CC BY-SA 4.0, https://commons.wikimedia.org/w/index.php?curid=77881429

- Pocahontas. By http://static1.wikia.nocookie.net/__cb20130523222621/disney/images/f/f2/Pocahontas_Disney.png, Fair use, https://en.wikipedia.org/w/index.php?curid=41776517

- Halloween 2010 in Austin Texas. By MarkScottAustinTX — https://www.flickr.com/photos/elchupacabra/5186129734/, CC BY-SA 2.0, https://commons.wikimedia.org/w/index.php?curid=81777670

- Members of the Native American Women Warriors, a Pueblo, Colorado-based association of active and retired American Indians in U.S. military service, at a Colorado Springs Native American Inter Tribal Powwow and festival in that central Colorado city. By Carol M. Highsmith, CC0, via Wikimedia Commons.

Navigating Change: Native American Women and the Columbian Exchange

- Two Tewa people processing wheat outside pueblo structure, San Juan Pueblo, New Mexico. Curtis, Edward S, photographer. Cleaning wheat — San Juan. San Juan Pueblo New Mexico, ca. 1905. Photograph. https://www.loc.gov/item/97507057/.

- 16th century Aztec drawing of smallpox victims. This smallpox epidemic struck the Aztec capital of Tenochtitlan in 1520 is taken from the Florentine Codex, a post conquest history written and illustrated by Aztec scribes. Viruses, Plagues, and History: Past, Present and Future, Oxford University Press, USA, p. 60 ISBN: 0–19–532731–4., Public Domain, https://commons.wikimedia.org/w/index.php?curid=12442514

- "America" by Theodor Galle (circa 1580) By After Stradanus — Americae decima pars, Public Domain, https://commons.wikimedia.org/w/index.php?curid=6499378

- Apsaroke woman on horseback, packhorse beside her. Curtis, Edward S, photographer. Pack horse i.e., packhorse — Apsaroke. Montana, ca. 1908. July 6. Photograph. https://www.loc.gov/item/2002722317/.

The Matrilineal Pueblo: Journeying Through the Lives of Pueblo Women in the Southwest from Pre-Contact to Colonization

- Photo shows women seated and standing on pueblo buildings. Curtis, Edward S, photographer. On the housetop — Hopi. Arizona, ca. 1906. December 19. Photograph. https://www.loc.gov/item/2002719490/.

- Curtis, Edward S, photographer. The Potter. , ca. 1906. Photograph. https://www.loc.gov/item/97503130/.

- Zuni woman kneeling on animal skin on floor, making pottery. Curtis, Edward S, photographer. Zuni Potter. New Mexico, ca. 1903. Photograph. https://www.loc.gov/item/94514442/.

- The mealing trough — Hopi, Pueblo. Curtis, Edward S, photographer. The mealing trough — Hopi. Arizona, ca. 1906. Photograph. https://www.loc.gov/item/92519541/.

- Tablita woman dancer — San Ildefonso, Pueblo. Curtis, Edward S, photographer. Tablita woman dancer — San Ildefonso. , ca. 1905. Photograph. https://www.loc.gov/item/96501822/.

- Pueblo Revolt 1680. By Loren Mozley for TRAP (USgov), 1936 — Derivative of File: First floor WPA mural at elevator at the U.S. Courthouse, Albuquerque, New Mexico LCCN2013634301.tif, Public Domain, https://commons.wikimedia.org/w/index.php?curid=129369574

Negotiating Power: The Influence of Native American Women in Fur Trading Roles in Early Northeastern America

- Photograph shows Native American Chippewa woman boiling syrup, probably maple syrup, on an open fire. Reed, Roland, photographer. Boiling Syrup. , None. [Between 1908 and 1912] Photograph. https://www.loc.gov/item/2020637525/.

- Photomechanical print is a copy of a lithograph "Chippewa Lodge," showing Native Americans constructing shelters. Lewis, Henry, Artist. Chippewa Lodge. Wisconsin, 1948. Photograph. https://www.loc.gov/item/2019630566/.

- Photocopy of ca. 1850 lithograph shows Native American women harvesting rice in birchbark canoe, indicating that the women are probably Chippewa. Eastman, Seth, Artist. Gathering Wild Rice. , 1948. Photograph. https://www.loc.gov/item/2020637512/.

- Tshusick, an Ojibwa woman, dressed in red and black, wearing medals and holding a flower Coloured Lithograph 1837 By: Charles Bird Kingafter: Alfred M. Hoffy and Thomas Loraine McKenneyPublished: 1837 By https://wellcomeimages.org/indexplus/obf_images/15/5a/a18f4f12c756453ff35b5535553c.jpgGallery: https://wellcomeimages.org/indexplus/image/V0047525.htmlWellcome Collection gallery (2018–04–01): https://wellcomecollection.org/works/kbjymt66 CC-BY-4.0, CC BY 4.0, https://commons.wikimedia.org/w/index.php?curid=36664139

- The Trapper's Bride, 1845. By Alfred Jacob Miller - http://www.liveinternet.ru/users/2010239/post111524817/, Public Domain, https://commons.wikimedia.org/w/index.php?curid=10478765

Revisiting Women's History: Decoding Bias in Champlain's Accounts of Huron Society

- Champlain. Butterfield, Consul Willshire, and Western Reserve Historical Society. History of Brulé's discoveries and explorations, -1626, being a narrative of the discovery, by Stephen Brulé, of lakes Huron, Ontario and Superior; and of his explorations the first made by civilized man of Pennsylvania and western New York, also of the Province of Ontario, Canada; with a biographical notice of the discoverer and explorer, who was killed and eaten by savages. Cleveland, Ohio, The Helman-Taylor company, 1898. Pdf. https://www.loc.gov/item/98002236/.

- 18th-century watercolor by an unknown artist. Artifact — Wendat Woman and Man (history.museum)

- Map of New France drawn by explorer Samuel de Champlain in 1612. geographique de la Nouvelle FrancePublic Domain, https://commons.wikimedia.org/w/index.php?curid=141988

- le grand conseil des femmes, chez les wyandot. By Élisée Reclus — Extrait de "L'Homme et la Terre", Public Domain, https://commons.wikimedia.org/w/index.php?curid=24469808

- The Miriam and Ira D. Wallach Division of Art, Prints and Photographs: Art & Architecture Collection, The New York Public Library. "Habit of a Wiendot woman. Femme Wiendot." New York Public Library Digital Collections. Accessed July 30, 2024. https://digitalcollections.nypl.org/items/510d47e4-81c0-a3d9-e040-e00a18064a99

- The Miriam and Ira D. Wallach Division of Art, Prints and Photographs: Picture Collection, The New York Public Library. "Bauern — Braut und Bräutigam, 1690" New York Public Library Digital Collections. Accessed July 30, 2024. https://digitalcollections.nypl.org/items/510d47e2-d13e-a3d9-e040-e00a18064a99

- Photo by Max-Jakob Beer on Unsplash

Iroquois Matriarchy: The Pinnacle of Female Political Power

- Drennan, Wm. A. , Copyright Claimant. Iroquois Indians. United States, ca. 1914. Photograph. https://www.loc.gov/item/2007661908/.

- George Catlin, Chée-ah-ká-tchée, Wife of Nót-to-way, 1835–1836, oil on canvas, 29 x 24 in. (73.7 x 60.9 cm), Smithsonian American Art Museum, Gift of Mrs. Joseph Harrison, Jr., 1985.66.197

- Plate 8. By New York State Museum — https://www.flickr.com/photos/internetarchivebookimages/14593343510/Source book page: https://archive.org/stream/annualreport6421910newy/annualreport6421910newy#page/n884/mode/1up, No restrictions, https://commons.wikimedia.org/w/index.php?curid=43167244

- Inside the Longhouse — IroquoianVillage, Ontario, Canada. The 15th century Iroquoian Village was reconstructed on its original site. By Laslovarga — Own work, CC BY-SA 3.0, https://commons.wikimedia.org/w/index.php?curid=24971119

- By Joseph François Lafitau (1681–1746) — Joseph-François Lafitau, "Customs of the American Indians compared with the customs of primitive times," 105., Public Domain, https://commons.wikimedia.org/w/index.php?curid=17616030

- Illustration shows Iroquois women on a rock overlooking women marching with banner labeled "Woman Suffrage". Includes brief text about the rights of Iroquois women. Keppler, Udo J., Artist. Savagery to "civilization" / Keppler ; drawn by Joseph Keppler. , 1914. New York: Published by Puck Publishing Corporation, 295–309 Lafayette Street. Photograph. https://www.loc.gov/item/97505624/.

The Real Pocahontas: Untangling Disney Myths, History, and Modern Native Women's Issues

- Pocahontas. By http://static1.wikia.nocookie.net/__cb20130523222621/disney/images/f/f2/Pocahontas_Disney.png, Fair use, https://en.wikipedia.org/w/index.php?curid=41776517

- Pocahontas Brings Food to the Colonists, 1906, par Elmer Boyd Smith. By Elmer Boyd Smith — http://onlinebooks.library.upenn.edu/webbin/gutbook/lookup?num=24487, Public Domain, https://commons.wikimedia.org/w/index.php?curid=55367128

- Smith, John, and Jay I. Kislak Reference Collection. The generall historie of Virginia, New England & the Summer Isles: together with The true travels, adventures and observations, and A sea grammar. Glasgow: J. MacLehose ; New York: Macmillan, 1907. Pdf. https://www.loc.gov/item/75320262/.

- Antonio Capellano Sandstone 1825 Capitol Rotunda, above west door By USCapitol - Preservation of Captain Smith by Pocahontas, 1606, Public Domain, https://commons.wikimedia.org/w/index.php?curid=21978308

- The Abduction of Pocahontas. She was an Algonquian princess in North America. Original Author: Johann Theodore de Bry after Georg Keller. Created: 1624 engraving, based on 1617 engraving. Medium: Engraving. By Johann Theodore de Bry after Georg Keller — Encyclopedia Virginia — https://encyclopediavirginia.org/7228hpr-eb1742f20ff08f1/ , the Virginia Historical Society, Public Domain, https://commons.wikimedia.org/w/index.php?curid=123289784

- Bell & Bro, photographer. Baptism of Pocahontas. , None. [Between 1860 and 1930] Photograph. https://www.loc.gov/item/2017652494/.

- Print showing large gathering of Natives and Englishmen for an outdoor wedding ceremony between Pocahontas and John Rolfe. Spohni, George, Lithographer, Anton Hohenstein, and Joseph Hoover. The wedding of Pocahontas with John Rolfe / Geo Spohni. , ca. 1867. Philadelphia: Published by Joseph Hoover, 719 Samson St. Photograph. https://www.loc.gov/item/2006677657/.

- Smith, John, and Jay I. Kislak Reference Collection. The generall historie of Virginia, New England & the Summer Isles: together with The true travels, adventures and observations, and A sea grammar. Glasgow: J. MacLehose ; New York: Macmillan, 1907. Pdf. https://www.loc.gov/item/75320262/.

- By United Artists — Private collection, CC BY-SA 4.0, https://commons.wikimedia.org/w/index.php?curid=112740779

- Activist action made at Pocahontas' memorial in St. George's Church, Gravesend, Kent, England, where her body is buried. The statue was covered with a black cloth, the official plaque was replaced for a new one, a pile of soil was placed in front of the statue and a fabric was extended on the ground which read 'LET'S BRING HER BACK HOME'. The activists demand Matoaka's body to be sent back to the land she came from (current Virginia, US) as they understand that her memorial in England is a symbol of colonial power that perpetuates the abusive treatment of the Native American nations. 2015. By Matoaka. Gravesend — Own work, CC BY-SA 4.0, https://commons.wikimedia.org/w/index.php?curid=44319206

BIBLIOGRAPHY

Anderson, Karen. "Commodity Exchange and Subordination: Montagnais-Naskapi and Huron Women, 1600-1650," *Signs* 11 (Fall 1985): 48-62.

Anderson, Marilyn J. "The Best of Both Worlds: The Pocahontas Legend as Treated in Early American Drama," *The Indian Historian* 12 (Summer 1979): 54-59, 64.

Axtell, James. *The Indian Peoples of Eastern America: A Documentary History of the Sexes* (1981).

Bataille, Gretchen M., and Laurie Lisa, eds., *Native American Women: A Biographical Dictionary* (New York: Taylor and Francis, Inc., 2nd ed., 2001).

Bruhns, Karen Olsen and Karen E. Stothert, *Women in Ancient America*, 2nd ed. (2014).

Buffalohead, Priscilla K. "Farmers, Warriors, Traders: A Fresh Look at Ojibway Women," *Minnesota History* 48 (Summer 1983): 236-44.

Dearborn, Mary V. *Pocahontas's Daughters: Gender and Ethnicity in American Culture*, Section 1. "A Case Study of American Indian Female Authorship," 12-30 (New York: Oxford University Press, 1986).

Evans, Sara M. Born for Liberty: A History of Women in America (New York, NY: Free Press Paperbacks, 1987, 1989).

Green, Rayna, "The Pocahontas Perplex: The Image of Indian Women in American Culture," *The Massachusetts Review* 16 (1975): 698-714.

Hubbell, Jay B., "The Smith-Pocahontas Story in Literature," *The Virginia Magazine of History and Biography* 65 (July 1957): 275-300.

Jennings, Matthew. *New Worlds of Violence: Cultures and Conquests in the Early American Southeast* (2011).

Lipman, Andrew. The Saltwater Frontier: Indians and the Contest for the American Coast (2015).

Medicine, Beatrice, "North American Indigenous Women and Cultural Domination," *American Indian Culture and Research Journal* 17 (1993): 121-30.

Mihesuah, Devon Abbott. Indigenous American Women: Decolonization, Empowerment, Activism. (Lincoln: University of Nebraska Press, 2003).

Powers, Karen Vieria, *Women in the Crucible of Conquest: The Gendered Genesis of Spanish American Society, 1500–1600* (2005).

Price, David A., *Love and Hate in Jamestown: John Smith, Pocahontas, and the Heart of a New Nation* (New York, 2003).

Richter, Daniel K. *The Ordeal of the Longhouse: The Peoples of the Iroquois League in the Era of European Colonization* (1992).

Rountree, Helen. "Powhatan Indian Women: The People Captain John Smith Barely Saw," *Ethnohistory* 45 (1998): 1-29.

BIBLIOGRAPHY

Sleeper-Smith, Susan, *Indian Women and French Men: Rethinking Cultural Encounters in the Western Great Lakes* (Amherst: University of Massachusetts Press, 2001).

The Voyages and Explorations of Samuel de Champlain (1604-1616). Narrated by Himself. (New York: A.S. Barnes & Co, 1906, and reprinted. Dartmouth, NS: Brook House Press, 2000).

Townsend, Camilla. *Pocahontas and the Powhatan Dilemma* (2004).

Waters, Frank. *Book of the Hopi* (New York: Penguin Books, 1982).

White, Bruce M. "The Wooman Who Married a Beaver: Trade Patterns and Gender Roles in the Ojibwa Fur Trade," *Ethnohistory* 46, no.1 (Winter 1999).

Young, Philip, "Pocahontas," *Portraits of American Women: From Settlement to the Present* (New York: St. Martin's Press, 1991): 13-33.

ABOUT ME

Dr. Agan is an adjunct professor of History at Modesto Junior College, where she has been a faculty member for over a decade. Her teaching expertise lies in women's studies and American history. Passionate about local history, she focuses her research on the environmental and social aspects of western settlement, particularly in the Central Valley. Dr. Agan's commitment to education empowers students to understand and appreciate the complex narratives that have shaped our past, while her forward-thinking approach inspires a brighter, more inclusive future.

Talitha Agan

TALLY NINE
Productions

Tally Nine Productions
tally9productions@gmail.com
Publishers Since 2022
Modesto, California

Agan, Talitha.
Her-Story Unveiled: Women's History
Through the Eyes of Native American
Resilience